Foundation Curriculum
Copyright © 2014
Written by Linda D. Washington
Illustrated by Rebeca Flott
Edited by Joyce S. Pace and Rita K. Jeffries

STORY BOOK LESSON 6
"THE KINGDOM OF GOD"

Jesus told us to pray and say,

"For Yours is the Kingdom,
and the Power,
and the Glory,
Forever.
Amen."

Let's see why Jesus wants us to pray
That the Kingdom, Power and Glory are God's Forever.

God, your heavenly Father, lives in a glorious Kingdom in heaven.

Father is pure love.

He has a royal law in His Kingdom.

Father's law is to love.

His Kingdom is filled with love, light, and life. The light comes from God. His love lights up all of heaven so there is no need for a sun.

His Kingdom is more magnificent than anything you can imagine.

Father rules the universe, the stars, the worlds, and all things from His Kingdom. Nothing or no one is more powerful than God, your Father.

God is Almighty!

Jesus lives with His Father in heaven. He is making big houses and places for Father's children to have fun there. In heaven, God has a River of Life that flows through the streets. There are bright colors and rainbows, gold and jewels, and friendly animals in heaven. Jesus has a horse that He likes to ride. Everything in heaven shows love and is alive. No one is sick. No one dies. There are no demons or devil to hurt anyone.

But on earth, people were sick. People died. And the devil and demons were hurting people. Earth was not like the Kingdom of God.

Father sent Jesus to change things on earth for good. Anyone who prayed and spoke from their heart that they believed Jesus, God made them His children. Father gave His children on earth the same power that He gave Jesus.

On earth, Jesus obeyed the Words His Father said. So Father called Jesus, The Word! Jesus talked to people and told them about His Father's Kingdom and how much Father loved them.

Jesus healed sick people because no one was sick in God's Kingdom. Jesus spoke to dead bodies and told their spirits to come back into their bodies because everything was alive in God's Kingdom. Jesus spoke and told the devil and demons to leave and quit hurting people. There were no demons or devil in heaven. As Jesus spoke Father's Words and did the things that Father told Him, Jesus was showing people on earth love, just like Father's Kingdom in heaven. What are some things that Jesus did to show people the Kingdom of God?

Jesus told people Father loves them.
Jesus healed the sick.
He made dead people come back to life.
Jesus spoke and told the demons and devil to stop hurting people and to leave.

Why do you think Jesus showed you what the Kingdom of God looks like?

Because Jesus wants you to show people the Kingdom of God also!

Jesus showed Father's Kingdom on earth and this made Father happy. Therefore, Father put power inside of the name of Jesus!

Listen to what the power in the name of Jesus can do. The power in Jesus name can make sickness leave. The power in the spoken name of Jesus can make dead people come back to life. The power in Jesus name can make the demons and devil leave. Jesus said whatever you ask in His name, He will do it and make it happen, so that Father may get glory in Him.

Jesus has chosen you because you believe Him. You are a child of God, a king and ambassador on earth for Jesus. He has given you the right to use His name to heal the sick, raise the dead, and make demons leave when you tell them to go away
in Jesus name.

Let's practice showing Father's Kingdom to heal someone. Think of someone who is sick. Ask if you can pray for them. If they say yes, tell them that Jesus loves them, and Jesus does not want them to be sick. Gently touch their body. Think about the power in the name of Jesus, and the super power of Holy Spirit on you and in you. Pray, and speak to the person's body. Say words like, "Be healed in Jesus name!" Then believe it is done, no matter what it looks like. Jesus said He will do it! Trust Jesus! Remember, it's not you healing the person. It is the power in the name of Jesus that heals them.

After you have prayed, always praise Father, and thank Him and Jesus for helping you to do His work! When you praise Father, He gets glory in Jesus. And since no one is sick in heaven, when you pray for someone who was sick, you have showed them God's Kingdom.

Why do you think Jesus wants you to pray and say that the Kingdom, Power and Glory is God's forever?

Jesus wants you to say it, because it is true. All the power belongs to Father! The words in this prayer, "For Yours is the Kingdom, and the Power, and the Glory, forever. Amen" has a mystery in it for you to solve, but you have to think and listen closely. Do you recall that Father called Jesus The Word? Did you know Father called someone else His Kingdom, Power, and Glory?

Let's find out who Father called His Kingdom, Power and Glory. You will get three clues.

Clue 1:

Jesus said the Kingdom of God is inside of you. Who did Father put inside of you when you were born again as His child? Holy Spirit! Father called Holy Spirit His Kingdom. Holy Spirit is on you and inside of you so God's Kingdom is in you.

Clue 2:

Jesus told people that Father would send His Power from heaven to live on them and in them. Who did Father send from heaven to live on and inside His children who believe Jesus? Father sent Holy Spirit! Father called Holy Spirit His Power! So the power of God is in you.

Clue 3:

Father said that He raised Jesus from the dead by His Glory. Who did Father call His Glory? Holy Spirit! Father called Holy Spirit His Glory. You carry the glory of God inside of you. And whenever you praise God, you give Father glory in Jesus.

Do you know why Father put His Kingdom, Power, and Glory of Holy Spirit in you?

Because Father chose YOU to show and tell everyone about His love and His Kingdom, just like Jesus!

The Purpose of the Foundation Curriculum

To firmly establish God's truth in each child's heart early in life so they will understand and know God's love and choose to live fully in the victory that Jesus Christ has already won.

The Goals

To show God's children his love, their true identity as children of God, their authority and power in Christ Jesus, their helper Holy Spirit, and how to pray to their Father in heaven.

THE KINGDOM OF GOD

Story Book Lesson 6

The Objectives to understand from "The Kingdom of God" are:

1. Father's Kingdom is full of Love.

2. Jesus obeyed His Father and showed God's Kingdom on earth.

3. Father called Jesus The Word.

4. Jesus spoke Words and healed the sick.

5. Jesus spoke Words and made dead people come back to life.

6. Jesus spoke Words and made the devil leave people.

7. Jesus gave you the power to speak in His name to do what He did and greater.

8. Holy Spirit helps you show Father's Power, Glory and Kingdom of Love to others.

P.A.C.E.
Products and Activities
for Christian Education

For Free Follow-Up Activities to Reinforce This Story Book Lesson Please Visit
www.ABC-Jesus.com

Biblical quotes were from different versions of the holy Bible.

Made in the USA
Middletown, DE
25 September 2021